Zoning 101

for Real Estate Agents

(and Clients)

An Introduction to Zoning and Land Use

By Alan O. Thompson

Definition of Land Planners

A group of people who sit in front of brightly colored maps and all hallucinate together.

I'm a Land Planner…

Land Planners….

…Hullucinating Together!

This book is designed for Real Estate Agents, their Clients, and anyone generally interested in the basics of zoning and land use. This is intended to be an introduction and is not an advanced comprehensive manual. There are plenty of other sources of advanced land planning information available.

Facebook: Zoning 101 for Real Estate Agents

SmartMAP.com
Intelligent Real Estate

Zoning 101 for Real Estate Agents (and Clients) by Alan O. Thompson. Published by:
Alan Thompson, LLC
5265 Sunset Lake Road, #40
Holly Springs NC 27540
www.SmartMAP.com

ISBN: 978-1-64316-394-9

Cover Design: pro_ebookcovers

Disclaimer: The information in this book is for informational purposes only. Everything mentioned herein should be verified with the appropriate agencies and responsible parties.

Zoning 101 for Real Estate Agents (and Clients)
By Alan O. Thompson
First Edition, July, 2018

THANK YOU

I want to thank my family, my friends, and my colleagues over the years who helped make me the person I am today. I must mention and thank my beautiful wife Maureen, our son Kurt, his beautiful wife Carrie, and our fabulous granddaughters, Emma, Olivia, Alexandra (Lexie) and Katarina (Katie), who are the reason Maureen and I now live in North Carolina!

TABLE OF CONTENTS

PREFACE

When I completed my military obligation in the 1970's and returned home, I had the option of going back to my previous State job or seeking new employment. I elected to take a new position that was offered to me by the local county. This was a position in the new county planning office.

The office had only been established a year earlier or so and was working on creating the first county zoning ordinance. An interim zoning ordinance had been put in place temporarily until the final ordinance could be created and adopted.

My first job was to help draw zoning boundaries on paper aerial photos. There were no property maps available at the time and we had to use physical features to create the proposed zoning boundaries. For example, we'd use tree lines assuming in most cases that this also would be the property line, or pretty close to it.

The final zoning ordinance had a provision stating that if a zoning boundary was near a property line, it was assumed the zoning boundary intent was to run along the property line. We also did "windshield surveys" driving around the county and marking land use on the aerial photos. We then used the newly completed Comprehensive Land Use Plan as a guide, along with the land use surveys, to determine the best we could what the appropriate zoning should be. This is when I was first introduced to what a Legal Nonconforming Use was.

Because of the lack of land use controls, land uses were often intermingled. Many existing commercial uses, for example, were then located in the new residential districts. These would then be allowed to continue in the residential districts as Legal Non Conforming Uses with certain restrictions that eventually would phase those businesses out of existence.

We eventually completed the final draft zoning ordinance and it went to a series of public hearings and was eventually adopted by the county council. That's when the real fun began!

County citizens, of course, were not used to being told what they could and could not do with their land. We were often called communists, etc. After that "baptism under fire" I spent an entire career in zoning and land use planning.

Of course, today, zoning is pretty much standard and accepted. Literally every jurisdiction has adopted zoning in one form or another. Those areas that do not have zoning ordinances usually have enough land use controls in place that pretty much produces the same result, controlled orderly development.

When I first became a Real Estate Broker, I noticed so many new Real Estate Agents had little understanding about zoning and land use, and the consequences it can have. To get a real estate license requires training and passing exams. Zoning and land use is covered in these classes and exams, but really just touches on this with all the other things that have to be taught and learned.

My goal in writing this book is to try and provide a basic understanding of zoning and land use law. As noted on the Introductory Page, this is intended to be an introduction to, and provide a basic understanding to help real estate agents effectively in their jobs. Very often, zoning is not an issue in standard residential real estate sales. But in many cases can be important to avoid problems. This includes understanding the difference between zoning regulations, HOA covenants, and deed restrictions. I have heard of agents who have lost their license after selling a home and the buyer not being able to what they intended and the agent had knowledge of that intent.

A basic understanding of zoning and its role in shaping local land use decisions, and the role of the **Planning Board** or **Commission**, **Board of Adjustment**, and **Council** (elected officials) in administering and implementing zoning is the goal.

Zoning is the way a community regulates the use of land. Zoning regulations allow a community to control where different uses occur and under what circumstances. Zoning groups land uses according to their compatibility and separates them to protect the health, safety and general well being of the community.

The authority to administer and implement local zoning is known as **Police Power**. This authority allows government, in protecting the public interest, to apply certain limitations to the use and development of land.

Zoning is a restriction of private property rights. As a result, it is subject to careful judicial scrutiny to see that the restriction is both legally necessary and reasonable. Zoning also includes restrictions in different zoning areas, such as height of buildings, use of green space, density (number of structures in a certain area), use of lots, and types of businesses, etc.

Zoning is based on a publicly adopted **Land Use Plan**, often called the **Future Land Use Plan** or **Comprehensive Plan**. This plan lays out the way the community wants to grow. So, if zoning is based on a plan, zoning then is the tool to implement that plan. To rezone a property, it must be in accordance with the adopted plan. If not, then the plan should be modified to match a desired zoning change.

Typically a Zoning Ordinance contains the complete set of zoning regulations. Recent trends combine the Zoning Ordinance and Subdivision Ordinance as well as other ordinances regulating land use into one comprehensive land use control ordinance typically called the **Unified Development Ordinance**, or **UDO**.

And finally, no land use determination is a slam dunk no matter what the ordinances say. Remember, land use controls are publically adopted by elected officials. In other words, it is often political.

What I mean is, not like the good old days when somebody's friends or wealthy contributor could push through poor projects for approval (I've actually seen that happen), but elected officials are often concerned about getting re-elected. I have had two multimillion dollar projects in two different states fail because the local jurisdiction declared moratoriums and a temporarily halt approving projects for various politically motivated reasons, although both projects were very sound, desirable, and keeping with the land use adopted ordinances.

Do your **Due Diligence** to understand the project you're working on and what to expect, and as Ronald Reagan once said, "Trust, but Verify!" That is verifying any advice and information with the proper authorities, including information in this book.

Alan Thompson
2018

"I'm from the City Zoning
Commission, sir — I'm afraid
that mustache will have to go."

CHAPTER ONE
Zoning 101

SmartMAP Zoning Map

SmartMAP.com
Intelligent Real Estate

Zoning 101 for Real Estate Agents

I'm a Real Estate Broker and Land Planner. I'm known in the office as the "Land Guy", primarily because I spent most of my career in Zoning Administration and Land Planning. Simply stated, zoning is the categorization of land by type of use and suitability. Most typical are Residential, Commercial, Industrial, Agricultural, Public Service, Preservation, and similar zoning districts. The purpose of zoning is the desire for orderly growth and compatibility with surrounding land uses as well as trying to achieve the highest and best use of the land.

I got a call from an agent in my office. She'd been an agent for two months and was still taking company training courses and had never had a sale. She had a call at the front desk out of the blue from a potential client who said he wanted stop in to sign a contract to purchase a property!!!

The client wanted to build a storage facility to house his personal car collection. The questions were: What kind of zoning was required? Could it be in a Residential District? If it's in a Commercial District, does it have to be open to the public? The answer was, it had to be in a Commercial or Industrial district, and no, it does not have to be open to the public. A storage building, or a garage, is an Accessory Building in a Residential District. An accessory building usually cannot be built in a Residential District without the Primary Use, a house! She found a Commercial/Industrial lot that served his purpose perfectly and she got her first sale!

Zoning is based on a Comprehensive Land Use Plan, often called General or Future Land Use Plan. In other words, how the jurisdiction envisions and/or wants future growth, and to best retain compatibility of existing land uses. These plans are publically adopted and therefore the general guidelines for future land use decisions. If the "Plan" is to be realized, then zoning is the tool to implement the plan.

Other things impact how the plan is created like soils, transportation, sewer, water and environmental considerations and suitability and compatibility. For example, a heavy industrial site may want rail access while a commercial site needs highway access. You also would not want a heavy industrial site next to a residential subdivision. The plan, and the zoning, tries to stay as contiguous and continuous when possible to protect other land uses and avoid "Spot" zoning.

Spot Zoning

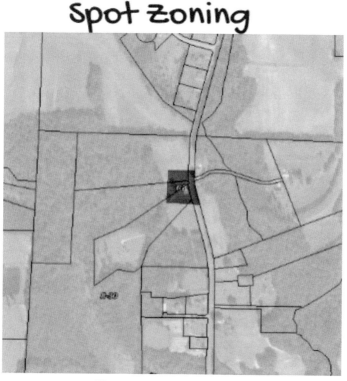

SmartMAP.com
Intelligent Real Estate

Spot Zoning is the application of zoning to a specific parcel or parcels of land within a larger different zoned area. The spot rezoning is usually at odds with the jurisdiction's Land Use Plan and current zoning restrictions. Spot zoning may be ruled invalid as an "arbitrary, capricious and unreasonable treatment" of a limited parcel of land by a local zoning ordinance. While zoning regulates the land use in whole districts, spot zoning makes unjustified exceptions for a parcel or parcels within a district.

Typically, each zoning district has permitted uses, accessory uses, prohibited uses, and uses requiring additional approvals such as a Conditional Use, Subdivisions, Site Plans, Schools, Churches, etc. Each zoning district has a primary use, or first permitted use.

An applicant applied for rezoning from Agricultural to Industrial. The stated purpose was a Fertilizer Blending Plant, which the applicant stated would support the surrounding Agricultural uses. The parcel was prime farmland and fronted on a highway. The Planning Staff recommended to the Planning Commission that the rezoning be denied because it was obvious Spot Zoning and the loss of a prime agricultural parcel. The staff recommended that the parcel be considered a Conditional Use, the Planning Commission endorsed the staff recommendation. The Council none the less approved the rezoning. The industrial site still exists today and a Fertilizer Blending Plant was never built. It is now a construction yard storing heavy construction equipment. It was Spot Zoning, against the Planner's recommendations, and resulted in the permanent loss of prime farmland. That Spot Zone will be there in perpetuity servicing heavy industrial use, surrounded by farms.

For example, a house in a residential zone is the primary use. Essentially, a primary use must be in place before secondary, or accessory structures are permitted. For example, you cannot build a garage in a residential zone without a house as the primary use of the property. However, in some cases, a garage or similar accessory structure may be allowed for temporary storage if the primary use, or house, is under construction.

Conditional Use A use that is allowed but because it has certain conditions that need to be added to minimize potential negative impacts.

Examples might be a fertilizer blending plant in an agricultural district. It might normally require Industrial zoning, but since it supports the agricultural industry, conditions are added to the plan to control various impacts. It also keeps the land zoned for agriculture and avoids Spot Zoning. If the plant ceases production at some future time, the Conditions of Approval for that particular use are no longer in effect. (See Sidebar on previous page).

A house is a first permitted use in a Residential district, but a residential subdivision will require additional approvals through the Subdivision Plan review procedures. While not technically a "Conditional Use", they are subject to conditions of approval from various regulatory agencies. Some Conditional uses may require Site Plan approval as well and many Commercial and Industrial uses.

Contract Zoning is a land use regulation where a local zoning authority accommodates a private interest by rezoning a district or a parcel of land within that district, on the condition that the limitations or restrictions set by the town for those parcels are accepted by the owner. The conditions are not necessarily applied to other similarly zoned parcels.

Courts have ruled contract zoning unconstitutional because the legislative body authorized to adopt zoning ordinances cannot delegate that power. The key distinction between illegal contract zoning and permissible conditional zoning is transparency of the public process and the extent to which the legislative body agrees to written specifics in the zoning ordinance. That is why you generally do not see a Site or Subdivision Plan at rezoning.

Another example of Conditional Use is a race track in a commercial zone. While a race track is certainly a commercial use, the character of a race track may produce noise, dust and parking & traffic issues that will need to be controlled by conditions.

In a case, a jurisdiction approved a race track as a permitted use with no conditions. The race track property was next to a wine vineyard that was well established and was very popular for weddings and other similar events. The owners of the vineyard filed a law suit against the race track and the jurisdiction because of the negative impacts that were going to be imposed on their property and business. A race track is clearly a conditional use and after a lot of angst, time and money, the court found in favor of the vineyard, which was obviously the correct finding.

Any use permitted in a zoning district is just that, permitted. An applicant can say what his intent is when requesting rezoning, but the jurisdiction cannot grant the rezoning based on intent. Once rezoned, the applicant can change their mind and put in any use permitted by that zoning district.

Performance Zoning is land use regulation based upon the application of specific performance standards represents an alternative to traditional zoning. Performance zoning provides for greater flexibility, avoiding the detailed specification of acceptable uses for specific parcels inherent in traditional zoning. It provides for the exercise of greater discretion by the regulatory jurisdiction at the time developments are proposed while at the same time establishing specific standards for the exercise of this discretion. This addresses many of the problems that have been identified with traditional zoning. The increased flexibility should also allow for land development and use to be more responsive to market forces, resulting in more economically efficient outcomes. Furthermore, performance zoning provides a framework for the establishment of a system for the exchange of certain rights that could allow for even greater responsiveness to the market.

Aesthetic Zoning The process of zoning a specific area to create a certain aesthetic look. Local zoning regulations are used to focus on the beauty of the community within its jurisdiction. The aesthetic zoning regulations are limited in nature, and must follow various guidelines designed to improve the appearance of the area and create a cohesive look.

The **Zoning Ordinance** is the adopted rules and regulations establishing zoning districts and uses. Today the Zoning Ordinance is often combined into the **UDO** (see next item).

Unified Development Ordinance (UDO) A single ordinance encompassing community uses, building including zoning, setbacks, architectural/aesthetic requirements, landscaping, signage and other development requirements for all property within the planning jurisdiction.

Official Zoning Map The map showing the location and boundaries of the zoning districts established by the jurisdiction.

Zoning Department The Planning Office and/or Community Development Department.

Zoning Inspector, The Zoning Inspector (or title as amended) of the Zoning Department, or designee thereof, and whose duties include administration and enforcement.

Zoning Certificate A document authorized by the Zoning Ordinance and issued by a Zoning Official authorizing a building or structure or the use of a building, structure, land or premises.

Zoning Certificate for a Sign A Zoning Certificate permitting erection, construction, reconstruction, enlargement, extension, moving or alteration of a sign.

Planned-Unit Development (PUD) Regulations that furthers the purpose of promoting the general public welfare, encouraging the efficient use of land and resources, promoting greater efficiency in providing public and utility services, and encouraging innovation in the planning and building of all types of development.

Mixed Use Zoning Districts allow for a combination of commercial and residential uses within a property, area or building. The commercial or residential portion of the development shall comply with the district regulations.

Overlay Zoning A zoning district overlapping another district. An example might be Historical Preservation District over a Residential District.

Height Restriction Restrictions on height of buildings based on the varying land use sand zoning districts.

Building Permit A permit issued by the Jurisdiction in compliance with the terms and provisions of the appropriate Building Code.

Building Code A set of regulations that specify the construction standards for buildings and structures.

Certificate of Occupancy A certificate indicating that a building or structure complies with the all applicable building codes.

Airport Flight Impact A pattern of aircraft routes set out by United States Government authorities to regulate the movements of aircraft and noise approaching or departing an airport.

SmartMAP.com
Intelligent Real Estate

CHAPTER TWO

Land Planning

Site Analysis

LAND PLANNING

This entire book could be called Land Planning 101 for Real Estate Agents because zoning and basically everything else discussed herein is an aspect of land Planning. I chose zoning because that is the tool to realize what land planning envisions. Zoning and restrictions on land use are most important to Real Estate Agents and can have the most immediate impact.

Land Planning literally means planning the land for its highest and best use, including for people, animals, development, and preservation to make the best use of the land in the most beneficial way for our planet.

It used to be that Land Planning was done by hand. Comprehensive Land Plans were often 20 year plans and the planners who worked on them might well be retired by the time the results were known. Today, that's not the case. Computers changed all that, but not without some growing pains. Prior to

A couple of years ago, my wife and I placed a deposit on a home along a golf course. It was a beautiful brick home and we were excited about getting it in such a wonderful location. We stopped by to look at it a few times as we were selling our old house. One bright and sunny day, as I walked on the lawn, the grass felt a little soggy! It had not rained for a while and I get immediately concerned.

I looked at the soils and sure enough, it had been built in Hydric Soils. Hydric Soils are poorly drained soil, in other words, Freshwater Wetlands!

I notified the Realtor, I was not one at the time, and withdrew our offer.

It was on a crawl space and I predicted it would have moisture issues. Sometime later, I drove by and saw a moisture mediation vehicle working on the crawl space.

It's not something most Real Estate Agents would know to look for, but you should be aware of this possible issue.

organized land planning, land use was basically random. All kinds of different land uses without any coordination and many things were built where they should have not been. One of the reasons why some developed areas often get flooded because they were built in low lying areas where they could not be built today. Lands were developed for years without consideration.

One of the important impacts on land development is the advent of Freshwater Wetlands Regulations. Freshwater wetlands did not used to be an issue in land development regulation. Homes, and often golf courses and other structures were built in freshwater wetlands as recent as the late 1980s, it just was not an issue. It is today however, and for all intents and purposes, you cannot, and should not, build in wetlands. These areas will be excluded from developable lands during project approval and engineering. Those wetland areas need to be identified, delineated, and, as mentioned, cannot be built on, or even disturbed for that matter. In addition, there are often minimum setback and buffer requirements. These areas are often not counted in overall developable acreage calculations.

Today, for land to be considered for development, a preliminary site analysis should be performed. It is essential to examine the pros and cons for development including sewer, water, soils, topography, wetlands as well as existing zoning and Land Plan recommendations.

In addition, a final site analysis will be accomplished, environmental impacts, and other considerations will be taken into account as final plans and engineering are accomplished.

I was an early adopter of PC technology. I wanted to make maps with planning information. I was told by the computer technicians at the time that you would never be able to make maps on a PC. The reason I was given that since a PCs programming language was BASIC, and FORTRAN was needed to make maps. Even though I knew pretty much nothing about computers at the time, I just refused to believe that. Of course, I've since spent most of my career making maps on PCs. I actually got a copy of AutoCAD, version 2. The first thing I did was to start digitizing planning information. As I created this information and was able to lay it over a map in the computer, there were conflicts of information. For example, one agency that had marked certain areas for preservation, another agency would have the same lands designated for development! With planners being able to see the results of their work instantaneously, this changed everything.

Maps by Author

Created by Hand

Created by Computer

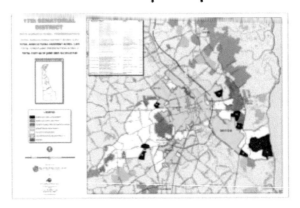

SmartMAP.com
Intelligent Real Estate

Agricultural Use Farming, ranching, horticulture, animal husbandry, including, but not limited to, the care and raising of livestock, equine, and fur-bearing animals and the production of poultry and poultry products, dairy production, the production of field crops, tobacco, fruits, vegetables, nursery stock, ornamental shrubs, ornamental trees, flowers, sod, mushrooms, timber, Also any combination of the foregoing; and the processing, drying, storage, and marketing of agricultural products when those activities are conducted in conjunction with, but are secondary to, such husbandry or production.

Agricultural Preservation Program Many jurisdictions are implementing formal agriculture preservation programs to protect undeveloped farmland. Tax incentives are offered for owners to enter into a program with the goal of purchasing the development rights and preserving farmland in perpetuity.

Farm A parcel of land usually 10 acres in size or larger primarily used for agricultural purposes, including farming, dairying, pasturing, agriculture, horticulture, animals and poultry and the necessary accessory uses for packing, treating or storing the produce, provided, however, that the operation of any such accessory uses shall be secondary to that of normal agricultural activities.

Federal Emergency Management Agency (FEMA) The Federal Emergency Management Agency is an agency of the United States Department of Homeland Security, initially created by Presidential Reorganization Plan No. 3 of 1978 and implemented by two Executive Orders on April 1, 1979.

Flood Insurance The specific insurance coverage against property loss from flooding. To determine risk factors for specific properties, Insurers will often refer to topographical maps that show lowlands, floodplains and floodways that aresusceptible to flooding

Flood Insurance Rate Map (FIRM) Flood zone areas that the FEMA has defined according to varying levels of flood risk. These zones are depicted on a community's Flood Insurance Rate Map (FIRM) or Flood Hazard Boundary Map. Each zone reflects the severity or type of flooding in the area.

Floodplain Low lying geographic areas that the Federal Emergency Management Administration (FEMA) has determined to be a flood risk to nearby communities and property.

When I was Planning Director, part of my job was to administer the Floodplain Regulations. I edited the provisions of our Zoning Ordinance with the FEMA requirements and the Council adopted the changes so we could amend the ordinance. Obviously I was well aware of the Floodplain requirements.

When we built our house, the lot we purchased was on a lake. The first thing I did was to check the FIRM Maps to make sure the property was not in a Flood Zone. It was not and we did not need Flood Insurance, so we built the house. We lived there for a number of years, with no problems.

Years later, we got a letter from our bank telling us we were required to buy Flood Insurance. This could not be possible, so I examined the maps again and found out they had been revised and the Flood Zones exaggerated.

We had to get a land surveyor to shoot elevations and submit to FEMA for a LOMA (Letter of Map Amendment). Took 6 months and some expense, but we did get our LOMA and did not need Flood Insurance.

One-Hundred Year Floodplain Any land susceptible to being inundated by water from a base flood. The base flood is the flood that has a one percent or greater chance of being equaled or exceeded in any given year. The 100-Year Floodplain shall be defined by the Federal Emergency Management Agency maps (FIRM).

Five-Hundred Year Floodplain The area of land susceptible to being inundated as a result of the occurrence of a 500-year flood. The 500-Year Floodplain shall be defined by the Federal Emergency Management Agency maps (FIRM).

Site Analysis A determination of how suitable a specific parcel of land is for a particular use. Typically a look at zoning, comprehensive plan recommendation, sewer, water, wetlands, soils, topography drainage, and anything that may affect the proposed use.

FIRM Map

SmartMAP.com
Intelligent Real Estate

Tax Map A map of a county, town, section or subdivision showing the location and boundaries of individual parcels of land subdivided into lots, with streets, alleys, easements, etc., usually drawn to scale.

Wetlands Lands transitional between terrestrial and aquatic systems where the water table is usually at or near the surface of the land and covered by shallow and/or seasonal water.

Freshwater Wetlands Generally areas saturated with water or covered by water at some time during the growing season each year, predominantly hydric soils, and/or wetlands vegetation.

Wetlands Delineation The flagging of wetland areas by a Land Surveyor or Engineer to mark wetland boundaries.

Boundary Survey A process carried out to determine property lines and define true property corners of a parcel of land described in a deed. It also indicates the extent of any easements or encroachments and may show the limitations imposed on the property by state or local regulations.

Board of Adjustment A committee which varies adopted regulations known as variances. They can also grant special exceptions and interpretations in the zoning regulations. Its decisions are final but may be subject to court action. The Board is appointed by the elected officials of the jurisdiction.

Variance Approved by the Board of Adjustment, grants the property owner relief from adopted regulations. Any variance granted by the Board of Adjustment must be based on the finding of an undue hardship caused by the strict application of the applicable ordinance. Such hardship must not be self imposed by the applicant.

Special Exception Similar to a Conditional Use because they have certain conditions that need to be added to minimize potential negative impacts. These are usually handled by the Board of Adjustment as opposed to the Planning Commission and Council.

Pre-Application, Scoping or Pre-Development Meeting A meeting between the applicant and staff of jurisdiction office to discuss the applicant's proposal for a proposed development.

Administrative Review A discretionary decision on a land use permit made by city or county staff without requiring a public hearing.

Planning Commission An appointed committee that reviews and makes recommendations to the Council on all proposals for rezoning, various development- related requests, and amendments   and additions to the jurisdictions zoning regulations comprehensive plan. The Planning Commission has no judicial or final decision authority but provides guidance to the Council.

Council A group of elected officials who come together to consult, deliberate, and make decisions relating to the jurisdiction. A member of a council may be referred to as a councilor or councilperson, or by the gender-specific titles of councilman and councilwoman, as well as commissioner.

Geographic Information System (GIS) A system designed to capture, store, manipulate, analyze, manage, and present spatial or geographic data. Typically assessment maps are on a jurisdiction website that allows access to view lots, aerials, assessment data and other information is a GIS.

Extra-Territorial Jurisdiction (ETJ) An area outside jurisdiction limits subject to jurisdiction zoning and building regulations. If property in the ETJ is developed, construction follows the jurisdiction's zoning and building regulations. This ensures, as property owners develop their lands, that the developments constructed on adjacent properties are harmonious with each other and with the jurisdiction's future land use plan. ETJ areas also allow the jurisdiction to manage infrastructure expansion (such as water and sewer lines) as lands are developed. Properties in the ETJ are not inside jurisdiction limits, and property owners do not pay jurisdiction taxes, but may be annexed.

Development Advisory Committee (DAC) A committee of technical consultants established to provide the planning office with technical assistance in the review of plans for compliance with the provisions of ordinances and other applicable rules and regulations of federal, state or local agencies.

Development Rights Properties have a certain development rights based on the zoning district in which it lies. Often, property owners have no desire to develop.

Development Rights, Transfer of (TDR) A voluntary, incentive-based program that allows landowners to sell development rights from their land to a developer or other interested party who then can use these rights to increase the density of development at another designated location. Agricultural Preservation programs often purchase development rights to permanently preserve farmland.

CHAPTER THREE
Subdivisions

Major Subdivision

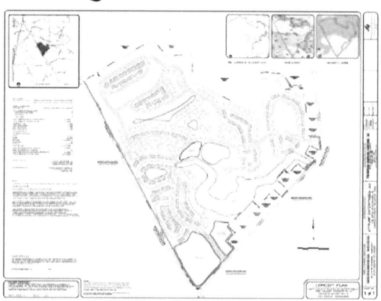

SUBDIVISIONS

Subdivisions come in many forms. These can be residential subdivisions, Industrial, business, condos, clusters, mixed use, PUDs, public, private, major, minor, etc. Subdivisions are simply the division of land into separate parcels.

The distinction of a **Major Subdivision** and a **Minor Subdivision** is that a major subdivision includes the opening of a street, or streets, and a minor subdivision does not and is merely just the dividing of a property into separate parcels. A minor subdivision usually has fewer lots than a major and fronts on an existing road or street. A major subdivision usually has a higher number of lots, and the approval process is more complex. Some jurisdictions allow Administrative Approval of minor subdivisions while a major will often require formal Planning Commission and Council meetings, public hearings and recommendations and approvals usually conditioned on certain requirements. All subdivisions usually require public recordation in a Recorder of Deeds, or similar office.

One misconception is that a subdivision does, in fact, usually consist of permitted uses in a zoning district. For example, a residential subdivision will consist of homes permitted in that particular residential zoning district and technically should not be denied if it meets all agency requirements and conditions of approval. I've sat on both sides of the fence, in the public sector and the private sector, where an unpopular project was approved. It's not a popularity contest as long as it meets all adopted requirements. I've had projects I didn't like and were certainly not popular, but they had to be approved. That is one reason why adopted regulations will from time to time be revised when certain flaws come to the attention of regulators. A rezoning of land to permit a certain kind of subdivision is a totally different story.

Subdivision The division of any tract of land into two or more plots, parcels, lots or sites for the purpose, whether immediate or future, of transfer of ownership or of building development.

A **Major Subdivision** Subdivisions which typically involve the creation and dedication of streets.

A **Minor Subdivision** Subdividing lots without an interior street.

Cluster Subdivision or **Clustering** A development pattern or design technique in which lots are grouped together, rather than spread evenly throughout a parcel as in traditional development. Clustering allows the remaining land to be used for outdoor active or passive recreation, open space, and the preservation of natural resources.

Traditional Subdivision A development option for new residential neighborhoods that provides a typical suburban form of residential development characterized by subdivisions of large/medium sized lots along curving streets. Sometimes call a Cookie Cutter Subdivision.

Minor Subdivision

SmartMAP.com
Intelligent Real Estate

CHAPTER FOUR

Land Uses

Principal and Accessory Structures

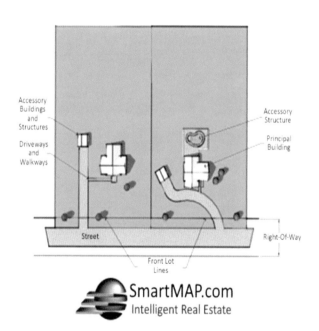

SmartMAP.com
Intelligent Real Estate

LAND USES

Land Use is basically the controlled orderly development and use
of land. The **Comprehensive Plan**, often called The General Land
Use Plan, designates areas that are the most suitable for certain
land use types. The Plan is the way the jurisdiction wants to grow.
As mentioned in other areas of this book, zoning controls land use
types and zoning is based on the Plan. This includes all land use in
the jurisdiction including preservation, farmland, parkland and so
on.

Typically, each zoning districts lists the land uses permitted,
density, setbacks, and other requirements. Each district will list
Permitted Uses (Primary), **Accessory Uses (Secondary)**,
Conditional Uses, and also in some cases, **Prohibited Uses**. There
are also **Legal Nonconforming Uses**, mentioned and defined in
this book. These uses do not conform to the current regulations for
various reasons. Primarily because they existed before adoption of
the current regulations and are **Grandfathered** In. a
nonconforming use may continue as is, but cannot be expanded
and should cease to exist at some point in the future. An example
of a legal nonconforming use might be a commercial use in a
residential district. The same can be said for legal nonconforming
signs and other structures. Lots can also be legal nonconforming
but probably won't be going away like a legal nonconforming use
might.

Normally, and **Accessory Use** cannot exist without a **Primary Use**.
The exceptions might be a garage in a commercial or industrial
zone, farm buildings, etc. Sometimes an accessory use like a garage
or shed might be allowed in a residential district as a Temporary
Use to store building materials and tools during construction of the
primary use. Upon completion of construction, the temporary
accessory use can become a permanent use.

A **Conditional Use** is one that is permitted with Conditions to
offset potential negative impacts on adjacent and surrounding land
uses.

Preservation and **Open Space** as well as **Buffer Areas** will usually not have developed land use. Although, depending on the preservation area, there may be some structures and buildings to support the area. Like **Nature Preserves**, fishing docks, observation towers, playgrounds and the like.

Home Occupations are another kind of land use. A home occupation is one that is run from a home in a residential community. The key to having a home occupation is to have no negative impact on the surrounding neighborhood. Many jurisdictions will have formal approval procedures and requirements for approval. Approval of home occupations is not as pertinent as it once was, before personal computers and Internet access. Now working from home has basically no impact on residential communities since working on a PC and accessing the Internet is not unlike watching TV. In fact, I am a proponent of Virtual Meetings and working from home reduces traffic congestion, pollution and gasoline consumption. I had a brick and mortar office in Delaware when I moved to North Carolina. I had some long term employees as well. I would drive back and forth between the two states for a couple of years. I eventually was able to close my expensive office, let my employees work from home, and communicated using the Internet and Video Conferencing just like we were sitting face to face. I was able to cut out the time and expense to travel, stay with my wife and see my Granddaughters, and my employees were happy. Our business continued until I retired. Since we did everything online, there was absolutely no impact on the residential neighborhood.

However, that all changes when you have clients coming in and out and/or storage of supplies, vehicles, etc. Professional Offices like a Doctor's office, engineering, architect, and similar professional services will require a formal home occupation approval. But these uses must still prove they will have minimal impact on the surrounding neighborhood.

Permitted Use A use that is allowed by right in a district after the issuance of a zoning certificate (in most cases), provided such use is authorized as a permitted use by the Zoning Ordinance. Each zoning district will have a list of permitted uses allowed by right. For example, houses in a residential zone, retail stores in a commercial zone, etc.

Prohibited Use A use that is not allowed in the specified district and in some cases the entire jurisdiction.

Temporary Use A use that is established for a fixed period of time with the intent to discontinue such use upon the expiration of such time.

Legal Nonconforming Use An existing use that is not compatible with the zoning district that it's in, but is legal, and "Grandfathered" in. This basically means when a zoning ordinance is adopted, there are usually existing uses which may continue because they predate an ordinance. Say, for example, a restaurant or convenience store located in a residential district. Basically it is intended that the use no longer exists at some point in time. Typically, a Legal Nonconforming use cannot be expanded and if such use closes down it can be used again only in conformity with the zoning ordinance. In some cases, jurisdictions will allow a nonconforming use of an equal or less intensive use than the original use.

Nonconforming Building or **Structure** A building, structure or parts thereof lawfully existing at the time the   Zoning Ordinance or a subsequent amendment became effective which does not conform to the requirements of the district in which it is located.

Substantial Reconstruction Any repair, reconstruction, or improvement of a structure, the cost of which equals or exceeds 50 percent of the market value of the structure either before the improvement or repair is started, or if the structure has been damaged and is being restored, before the damage occurred. Substantial reconstruction is considered to occur when the first alteration in any way, ceiling, floor, or the other structural part of the building commences, whether or not that alteration affects the external dimensions of the structure. The term does not, however, include either any project for improvement of a structure to comply with existing state or local health, sanitary specifications, which are solely necessary to ensure safe living conditions, or any alteration of a structure listed on the National Register of Historic Places or a state inventory of historic places.

Nonconforming Lot A lot legally established prior to the effective date of a Zoning Ordinance which does not meet the standards of the district in which it is located. This can involve minimum area, or dimensional requirements of the lot.

Principal Use (Primary Use) The main use to which a parcel, lot, or premise is used. For example, a house is the primary or principal use in a residential district.

Secondary Use (See **Accessory Use**) Allowed as long as there is a primary structure. See **Primary Use**. A garage, shed, or other outbuildings would be secondary structures to the primary use of a residential property.

Principal Structure (Primary Structure) means the main structure for the zoning district in which the property is located.

Accessory Use A use incidental to and customarily associated with a specific principal or primary use, located on the same lot or parcel.

Accessory Structure A structure which is on the same parcel of property as a principal or primary use or building the use of which is incidental to the use of the principal use or building (such as gazebos and carports).

Structure Anything constructed or erected, the use of which requires a location on the ground or is attached to something having a location on the ground, and includes, but is not limited to, buildings, parking lots, driveways, sidewalks, fences, seating facilities, platforms, backstops, pergolas, ponds, pools, poles, tanks, tents, towers, transformer substations, signs, walls, canopies, air supported structures, street gutters, detention basins, extended detention basins, retention basins, constructed wetland infiltration basins, catch basins, oil/water separators, sediment basins, modular, porous and solid pavements, and aggregate stone driveways. Structure also includes any edifice used for storage.

Child Day-Care Center Any place in which child day-care is provided, with or without compensation, multiple children at one time or any place that is not the permanent residence of the licensee or administrator in which child day-care is provided.

Comprehensive Land Use Plan Zoning is based on a publically adopted plan, typically called a Comprehensive and/or Land Use Plan. The plan shows areas where the jurisdiction would like certain land use types and growth to happen. Zoning then is the "tool" to realize the Plan.

Home Occupation An occupation conducted within a dwelling on a lot within a residential zoning district, or as an accessory use of a dwelling for an occupation, profession, enterprise or activity conducted by a family residing on the premises which is clearly incidental and secondary to the use of the premises for dwelling purposes. Home occupations typically do not impact the neighborhood and generally are not allowed if:

1. It changes the outside appearance of the dwelling or is visible from the street.
2. Generates traffic, parking, utility use in excess of what is normal in the neighborhood
3. Creates objectionable noise, smoke, fumes, odor, dust or electrical interference; or
4. Results in outside storage or display of anything.

Plat A map (site plan, survey), drawn to scale, showing the development, boundary and/or divisions of a piece of land. Typically when a project is approved, a final plat is required to be recorded in the Recorder of Deeds Office.

CHAPTER FIVE

Lots

Building Setback Requirements

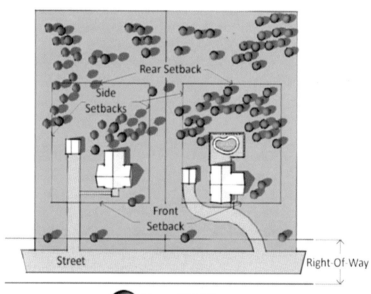

LOTS

Everyone in the United States is familiar with lots. It's one of the basics of our way of life and economy. Lots, of course come in all types and sizes. Lots can be residential, commercial, industrial, open space, preservation, public service, and so on.

A farm or large piece of land or acreage is not usually referred to as a lot, but of course their characteristics are the same, just a larger parcel serving a particular use. All lots will have certain characteristics like building setbacks, buildable area requirements and use based on the zoning district in which it is located. Also, lot area requirements may vary for numerous reasons including utilities access, or lack thereof.

Passive Open Space, **Recreation** and **Buffer Areas** that will not be built on will not have these restrictions. **Active Open Space** and **Recreation Areas** that will have structures and parking areas will have minimum setbacks and other requirements.

A typical development lot will have, among other requirements, front, side and rear setback requirements, also referred to as Yards, such as **Front Yard**, **Rear Yard** and **Side Yard**. These setbacks will determine **Buildable Lot Area**. Some jurisdictions will define the Front Yard as the line along the front of the primary structure, such as a house. So if the minimum front setback is 40' and the front of the house is 70' back, they define that as the front yard line. I've always maintained, and wrote in our ordinances that that was not the case, and the minimum front yard setback remains what the ordinance requirements indicate it is. Having said that, we had other requirements to insure that an accessory structure, like a shed, for example, could not be located in front of a house. This then would not restrict an attached garage to be constructed if it did not have to be the same exact setback, or more, as the house.

A farm, of course, with out buildings, etc, would not have this issue. These things, as stated and emphasized already in this book, need to be verified by the regulatory agencies having jurisdiction over these properties.

Lot A parcel of land of sufficient size to meet minimum zoning requirements for use, coverage and area, and to provide such yards and other open spaces. Such lots shall have frontage on an improved public or private street or have access to a legal right of way and shall be a lot of record.

Lot Coverage The ratio of gross floor area of all buildings and structures and all areas that are associated with driveways and parking areas on a lot to the total lot area, expressed as a percentage.

Lot of Record A lot which is part of a subdivision recorded in the office of the county recorder, or a lot or parcel described by metes and bounds, the description of which has been so recorded, and is shown as a separate unit on the last preceding county tax roll.

Lot Width The distance across the lot (side lot line to side lot line), measured in conformance with the provisions set out in the Zoning Ordinance.

Buildable Area The area of a lot remaining after the minimum yard and lot area requirements have been met and in which development may occur subject to compliance with all applicable development standards.

Frontage The boundary between a plot of land or a building and the road onto which the plot or building fronts. Frontage may also refer to the full length of this boundary.

Lot Line The boundary of a lot separating it from adjoining public or private land, or the dividing line between lots, pieces or parcels of land, without regard to any recorded subdivision plat.

Front Lot Line The lot line which abuts a dedicated street, private road or easement of access. Typically a lot owner can designate the front lot line for any corner lot or through lot and such designation may not be changed after the principal building is erected.

Rear Lot Line For a **quadrangular lot**, the lot line which is not tangent to any point on the front lot line. For a **polygonal or irregularly shaped lot**, the course, whether straight or curved, along the lot line, the center point of which is most remote, in linear distance, from the center point of the front lot line. For a **triangular lot**, the junction point of the two side lines which point shall be treated as the rear lotline.

Side Lot Line The lot lines that run generally perpendicular or at angles to the street or any lot line which is not a front or rear lot line.

Deed Restrictions Private agreements that restrict the use of the real estate in some way, and are listed in the deed. The seller may add a restriction to the title of the property. Often, developers restrict the parcels of property in a development to maintain a certain amount of uniformity.

Front Yard A yard of uniform depth extending the full width of the lot between a principal structure erected thereon setting back from and nearest such street line. In the event that a yard along the front street line and the parts of the fronts on a denied-access road, such yard shall not be considered a front yard.

Rear Yard A yard of uniform depth across the full width of the lot extending from the rear line of the principal structure to the rear line of the lot.

Side Yard A yard between the building and the adjacent side line of the lot and extending from the front yard to the rear yard.

Impervious Surfaces Areas including streets, driveways, parking lots, rooftops and similar areas that water cannot infiltrate. In some cases, soils compacted by development can also be impervious.

CHAPTER SIX
Housing Types

SmartMAP.com
Intelligent Real Estate

HOUSING TYPES

The many housing types are dependent on the zoning district in which it is located. Various jurisdictions will have various permitted housing types outlined in its regulations. Anything from conventional single-family detached homes, attached, semi-detached, to multi-family, manufactured, modular, cluster, zero lot line, patio, group, multi-generation, tiny homes and so on. These housing types are defined in this chapter so I won't repeat them here. Some housing types, and size may be sometimes determined in deed restrictions.

Often, **Mixed Use** or **Planned Unit Developments (PUD)** will have several housing types and a minimum percentage requirement of homes and types verses neighborhood commercial uses, open space, etc. All the setbacks and other requirements will also be met. In some cases, residential development will be built behind shopping centers and often use higher density homes and buffers near the commercial areas, transitioning to lower density residential. Often these residential areas will take access through the commercial areas as well as other secondary access.

Cluster Development will often allow homes to be "clustered" on a smaller area of the site while maintaining the same permitted overall density. This allows more **Open Space** areas and enhances the esthetics and the community's use of land. This may well include different housing types to more efficiently locate the homes in a smaller area.

28 out of 38 acres preserved as open space

Single-Family Detached Dwelling units that are located in individual buildings that are constructed on individual lots intended for the use of a single housekeeping unit.

Single-Family Attached Two or more dwelling units that are designed so that individual units have individual ground-floor access and are separated from each other by common walls from foundation to roof. Two dwelling units that are designed so that individual units may or may not have individual exterior doors, but provide no direct access between the first floor and second floor unit (access may be through a common interior foyer that provides access to both units or through separate exterior doors) and are separated from each other by a floor (e.g., over-under duplexes).

Patio Home or **Cluster Home** A house typically in a suburban setting, part of a unit of several houses attached to each other, typically with shared walls between units, and with exterior maintenance and landscaping provided through an association fee.

Townhouse A single-family dwelling unit constructed in a row of attached units separated by a common wall and property lines.

Weak-Link Townhouse The term "weak-link townhouse" means that the units share a common wall, but each unit has a one-story and two-story section. Oftentimes, this makes the weak-link townhouse wider than a standard townhouse.

Zero Lot Line Home A piece of residential real estate in which the structure comes up to or very near to the edge of the property line. Row houses, garden homes, patio homes and townhomes are all types of properties that may be zero-lot-line homes. They may be attached (as in a townhome) or detached, single story or multistory.

Manufactured Home (HUD Code) A single-family dwelling unit fabricated in an off-site manufacturing facility bearing a label certifying that the unit is built in conformance with Federal Manufactured Housing Construction and Safety Standards (24 CFR 3280), transportable in one or more sections which, in the traveling mode, is eight feet or more in width, or 40 feet or more in length, and built on a permanent chassis designed for use with or without a permanent foundation when connected to the required utilities.

Tiny homes can be a difficult issue. Recently a church wanted to place a number of tiny homes on their property to house homeless veterans. Who can argue with such a good cause?

However, when they applied for permits from the county to place the homes, they were denied. Basically, the placement of tiny homes would constitute a subdivision, which requires a subdivision plan review and approval. Also, there are many requirements including public hearings, central water and sewer, electric, streets, drainage and numerous other approvals.

Unfortunately, this is not just regulations getting in theway, but important issues to the health safety and Welfare of the community and its citizens.

Although a good idea in theory, just not a practical reality.

Modular Home (BOCA Code) Modular buildings and Modular Homes are sectional prefabricated buildings, or houses, that consist of multiple sections called modules. The building method is referred to as permanent Modular construction. Modular Homes are built the same and considered the same as a stick built Homes.

Duplex Home A house having separate living units for two families, especially a two story house having a complete living unit on each floor and two separate entrances.

Twin Home A single building on a single lot, which contains two dwelling units, each of which is totally separated from the other by an common wall extending from foundation to roof.

Multi-family Buildings that contain three or more dwelling units and are accessed from interior elevators or hallways, or from individual exterior entrances. They are also separated by interior walls and/or floors. Multi-family does not include boarding houses, dormitories, fraternities, sororities, bed and breakfast establishments, single-family attached or overnight accommodations like hotels and motels.

Condominium A form of real property ownership in which a declaration has been filed submitting the property to the condominium form of ownership under which each owner has an individual ownership interest in a unit with the right to exclusive possession of that unit and an undivided ownership interest with the other unit owners in the common elements of the condominium property.

Multigenerational Home A single-family home consisting of more than two generations living under the same roof. They generally include separate living quarters including a main kitchen and kitchenette. The kitchenette as opposed to two kitchens differentiates a multigenerational home from a multi-family home.

Tiny Home Houses of less than 1,000 square feet. Frequently, the distinction is made between small houses, 400 square feet to 1,000 square feet, and tiny houses, less than 400 square feet, with some as small as 80 square feet.

CHAPTER SEVEN
Streets

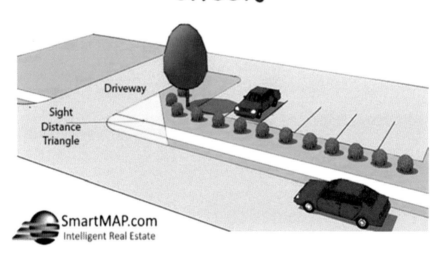

STREETS

Streets come in many configurations, size and functions. The opening of streets defines a Major Subdivision from a Minor Subdivision, which fronts on an existing road and does not involve interior street construction.

Streets can be public or private, paved or unpaved, full access or limited access, local or thoroughfare, and so on. A Public Street is one that is dedicated to public use and maintained by the responsible public agency or jurisdiction. It uses revenue from taxes and/or tolls. A **Private Street** will be maintained by the property owners abutting and using the street, sometimes through a **Homeowners' Association (HOA)**. This will often be referenced on a plat or survey of the community and recorded in a **Recorder of Deeds Office** or similar agency. Sometimes private street maintenance will be outlined in the deed restrictions for a property. Similarly, public street maintenance responsibility will be indicated on a plat or survey publically recorded. Depending on the responsible jurisdiction, construction standards and requirements may be differ for public streets and private streets.

An often misunderstood aspect of streets and roads is the **Right of Way (ROW)** width. It usually exceeds the physical roadway width. For example, a roadway surface may be 22' in width, but the ROW may be 50' or 60 wide', and sometimes more, most particularly on a public street or road. The ROW on a public street is the area **Officially Dedicated to the Public Use**. The ROW is for road maintenance, potential future expansion and utilities and other things supporting the road and/or surrounding properties. In a residential subdivision with public streets, for example, the ROW typically will include sewer and water lines, drainage structures, other utilities including poles, signs, sidewalks, grass and trees and curbing. Even though these areas are dedicated to public use, the property owner is responsible for cutting the grass and trees, shoveling sidewalks, etc. This may vary in a condominium or HOA regulations.

Typically, telephone poles along a roadway will be placed on the outer edges of the ROW, making the width of the ROW easier to discern.

Building setbacks discussed and defined in other areas of this book begin at the ROW boundary line, not the **Edge of the Pavement (EOP)**, curbs, or sidewalks.

Older deeds, surveys and plats will often define a property boundary to be at the center of a road. Original acreage calculations were based of those boundaries. Since new roads and ROWs have been established since those deeds and surveys were created, the acreage calculation is reduced from the original figures.

Street Land, comprising the entire area within a street right-of-way, which is intended for use as a means of vehicular and pedestrian circulation, which provides access to more than one lot.

Right-of-Way (ROW) An area dedicated to use, either public or private, for the purpose of vehicular and/or pedestrian travel and/or access.

Street, **Public** A publicly dedicated, accepted and maintained right-of-way, open to the general public for the purposes of vehicular and pedestrian travel affording access to abutting property. A public street may be comprised of pavement, shoulders, gutters, curbs, sidewalks, parking spaces, and similar features.

Street, **Private** A privately-held and maintained right-of-way open to the general public for the purposes of vehicular and pedestrian travel affording access to abutting property, whether referred to as a street, easement, road, expressway, arterial, thoroughfare, highway. A private street may be comprised of pavement, shoulders, curbs, sidewalks, parking spaces, and similar features.

Street, Cul-de-Sac A local street having one open end and being permanently terminated at the other by a vehicular turnaround.

Street, Frontage A street located along side and generally parallel with a more heavily traveled street and which provides access to abutting properties.

Street, Local A street primarily designed and intended to carry low volumes of vehicular traffic movement at low speeds within the immediate geographic area with direct access to abutting properties.

Street, Loop A type of local street each end of which terminates at an intersection with the same arterial, collector, or local street.

Street, Limited Access A street along which access is restricted due to the acquisition of access rights from adjoining properties by the appropriate governmental agency having jurisdiction over such street.

Street, Marginal Access A local or collector street providing access to abutting properties and protection from arterial or collector streets.

Street, Collector A street or road for through traffic movement, which intercepts traffic from intersecting local streets and directs traffic movement to the nearest arterial street, typically carrying medium traffic volumes. A secondary function is providing access to abutting property.

Street, Thoroughfare A street designated as a thoroughfare is a main road with stores and heavy traffic.

Street, Freeway A street designated as a freeway (highway) with controlled access.

Street, Arterial A street or road for through traffic movement, typically carrying heavy traffic volumes, usually on a continuous route. A secondary function is providing access to abutting property.

Street, Sight Distance (Daylight Corner) The triangular area formed by a diagonal line connecting two points located on intersecting street right-of-way lines, or a right-of-way line and the curb or edge of a driveway for the purpose of providing clear visual access. (See Chapter Graphic)

Alley, Private A private right-of-way for public use as a secondary means of public access to a lot abutting a public or private street and not intended for traffic other than public services and circulation.

Alley, Public Any public right-of-way which has been dedicated or deeded to and accepted by the public for public use as a secondary means of public access to a lot abutting a public street and not intended for traffic other than public services and circulation.

CHAPTER EIGHT

Easements

Easements

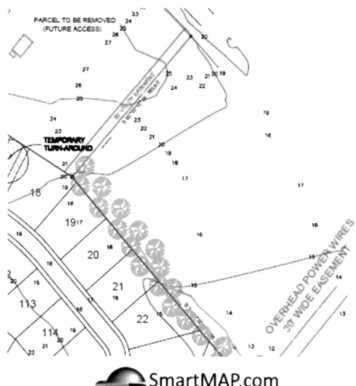

SmartMAP.com
Intelligent Real Estate

Easements

Easements serve many purposes. One of the most common easements that most of us are familiar with are **Utility Easements**, often seen with overhead utility lines. Today, especially in subdivisions, utility easements are not easily seen since the utilities will be placed underground. Right of Ways (ROWs), as discussed in Chapter 7, are easements including utilities.

Access Easements can serve as a private street serving one or several parcels of land, particularly in older deeds and plat predating current modern regulations. Access easements have been used to provide access to landlocked parcels. It is my understanding that in Delaware, where I used to work and one of the original 13 Colonies, that access to a landlocked parcel has the right to access the property over the parcel that caused it to be landlocked. Not sure if this is old English law but I've never seen it in writing and it was never an issue I had to deal with.

I have dealt with what are called **Pipestem Lots**, or sometimes called **Flag Lots**. These lots were allowed in older ordinances, but not so much now. Basically they are shaped like a pipe stem or a flag, hence their names. Often, minimum **Road Frontage Width** was smaller than the minimum lot width. **Minimum Lot Width** is different than minimum lot width and this would allow an access easement over a smaller strip of land to a larger part of the parcel where a house could then be built. This could be to one parcel or several parcels. For example, minimum road frontage may have been 25' while the minimum lot frontage may have been 100'. Typically, the 25' strip would be a driveway leading back to a house. With multiple lots, this might be shared driveways of 25' each with **Cross-Access Easements** serving the lots, or basically, a private road, and would also be a minor subdivision. A maintenance agreement may or may not exist. A real estate agent should be aware of what these are since once they are in existence, they most likely will remain in existence, even if they are not allowed today.

Pipestem Lots

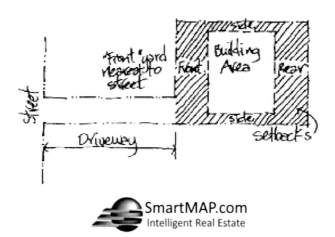

Many easements will be shown clearly on plats and surveys, and some are shown on Parcel Maps (Tax Maps). Some need to be researched and many in deeds. There are many more types of easements and many are defined in this Chapter. This is not legal advice and often an Attorney can research and clarify these. There are also other references available that offer more clarity and information.

Access Easement A recorded private easement for vehicular access across one lot or parcel to another (for example a driveway across a lot to access another lot). Cross-access easements are reciprocal arrangements that provide for the free flow of vehicles across the property line of abutting lots (for example a driveway connection between abutting non-residential uses).

Easement A non-possessory right to use and/or enter onto property of another. The easement may be Condemnation where government exercises eminent domain or the land is officially condemned.

Easement, Express Grant An easement may be created by an express grant or reservation. An express grant of an easement is made by way of a written deed signed by the grantor. An express reservation is made when a grantor of real estate reserves an easement in the deed he uses to convey the real estate.

Easement by Necessity Allows an owner of a landlocked parcel to cross over another's land to access a public road. Easements by Necessity are known as Appurtenant. This means that they benefit a particular piece of land, rather than an individual person.

Easement Appurtenant Attaches to the land permanently and benefits its owner. In order for it to exist, there must be two pieces of land owned by different individuals. One piece, the Dominant Estate or Tenement, is the land that is benefited by the easement. The other piece, known as the Servient Estate or Tenement, is the land that has the burden of the easement. An Easement

Appurtenant is a Covenant running with the land since it is

incapable of a separate and independent existence from the land to which it is annexed.

Easements by Prescription Acquired by hostile, open and notorious use for five years. For example, prescriptive easements could be claimed by a person who travels across a parcel of land owned by another and continuously for five years without the owner's permission or consent.

An **Easement in Gross** Not appurtenant to any estate in land. It arises when a Servient piece of land exists without a dominant piece being affected. This type of easement is ordinarily personal to the holder and does not run with the land.

CHAPTER NINE
<u>Buffers & Preserved Lands</u>

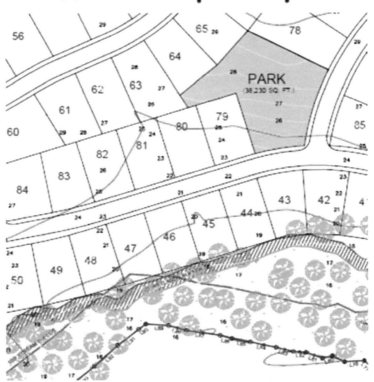

SmartMAP.com
Intelligent Real Estate

BUFFERS & PRESERVED LANDS

Buffers and Preserved Lands are a part of pretty much all modern day land use controls. Often Landscape Buffers are required between certain land uses. **Neighborhood Open Space (NOS)** is required in most residential subdivisions. These Open Space Areas can be Passive or Active. Many communities today are requiring Greenway connections that provide natural access for walking, running and bicycling.

Passive and **Preservation Open Space** will often not have any structures, although some may for minimum preservation needs. Passive open space would be parkland, forest lands and nature preserves, as well.

Active Open Space might include playgrounds, athletic fields, park and preserves. Many open space areas are required by the local jurisdiction, however, there are also protected lands at every level including private, State, County, as well as Federally protected lands.

Buffers are often landscaped or vacant open areas, however buffers can also be various land uses, such as higher density buffering to lesser density development. For an example, today, in least in my area, homes are being built behind shopping centers. The homes will often start with high density residential, such as apartments, condos, or townhouses. It will then transition into lower density development such as larger townhomes, and then single-family detached homes.

Preserved Lands may be public utility uses, drainage areas, steep areas, historic properties and others depending on local areas and conditions. This, of course, would include environmentally sensitive areas such as lakes, ponds, wetlands and setback and buffer areas.

Buffer Zone A tract of land between two differently zoned areas. For example, a city might position open space between a commercial and residential district by including buffer zones like parks, gardens and riding trails.

Buffer Open spaces, landscaped areas, fences, walls, berms, or any combination thereof, which are used to physically and visually separate one use or property from an abutting property in order to mitigate the impacts of noise, light, or other nuisance.

Buffer Yard A designated strip of land upon which a buffer is installed. Buffer yards may be required between land uses, along district boundaries, along parking lot boundaries, and along street and railroad rights-of-way.

A golf course community was proposed on a prime piece of farmland in an agricultural community. The current agricultural zoning district allowed the proposed use including residential one acre lots. However, the developers desired higher density and applied for rezoning to another zoning district that allowed 1/2 acre residential lots. The rezoning caused controversy and the night of the Planning Commission public hearing, there was a standing-room-only crowd.

It was announced before the hearing began that the applicant had withdrawn the application. The reason was a provision in the zoning ordinance that allowed 3/4 Acre residential lots with the dedication of Neighborhood Open Space (NOS). When the final plan was recorded, the applicant dedicated the golf course permanent neighborhood open space.

This allowed a successful project and avoided a controversial rezoning that would have created a spot zone, although a very large one.

Outdoor Public Recreation, Active The public use of public property to provide active recreational facilities for the community within a park-like setting and atmosphere; to promote certain healthy and beneficial outdoor leisure time activities for park users which do not present a significant risk of harm to others; and to afford reasonable access for the public to outdoor athletic, social and educational activities. Compatible uses are intended to be active in nature and will require modification and alteration of natural terrain and disturbance to natural habitat to create a balance between the public's need for active outdoor recreation and preservation of open space.

Outdoor Public Recreation, Passive The public use of public property to protect and preserve park lands, wilderness areas, open spaces, and scenic areas to conserve fish and wildlife, to promote forestry, wetlands, and other natural habitats and to promote natural green spaces for the community to use for passive recreational purposes. Compatible uses are intended to be passive in nature to prevent the disturbance of the natural terrain, habitat and wildlife. Public open space is designed and intended for common use and the enjoyment of the residents. Open space is sometimes referred to as "green space".

Neighborhood Open Space (NOS) A land area that will be left undeveloped as part of a natural resource preservation, recreation, buffer yard, or other open space provision of a zoning ordinance or UDO. Open Space excludes the residential areas in lots, street rights-of-way, or parking lots. Private open space is designed and intended for common use and the enjoyment of the residents of a subdivision or other residential development.

Protected Lands Lands permanently protected from development, whether by purchase or donation, through a perpetual conservation or open space easement or fee ownership for their cultural, historical, ecological, or agricultural value.

Riparian Area Naturally vegetated land adjacent to watercourses that, if appropriately sized, helps to stabilize stream banks, limit erosion, reduce flood size flows, and/or filter and settle out runoff pollutants, or performs other functions consistent with the purposes of this regulation.

Riparian Setback Lands that fall within areas defined by the criteria set forth in applicable ordinances to avoid encroachment by allowable structures.

Stormwater Management For water quantity control, a system of vegetative, structural, and other measures that may control the volume and rate of stormwater runoff which may be caused by earth disturbing activities.

Retention Basin A facility for the collection and release of surface and stormwater runoff from a site at a slower rate than it is collected by the drainage facility system, the difference being held in temporary storage. A retention Basin is also a facility within which stormwater runoff is stored in a permanent pool of water, sometimes referred to as a wet pond.

Soil and Water Conservation District An entity organized referring to either a Soil and Water Conservation District Board or its designated employees.

Soil Disturbing Activity The clearing, grading, excavating, filling, dumping, grubbing, stripping, or other alteration where natural or human made ground cover is destroyed and which may result in, or contribute to, erosion and sediment pollution.

Sedimentation The accumulation of soils or other surface materials transported and/or deposited by the action of wind, water, ice, or gravity as a product of erosion.

Waste Water Treatment Plant A facility at the end of a sanitary collection system which processes waste, and discharges water to a receiving system, treated to the standards of the Environmental Protection Agency (EPA)

CHAPTER TEN

<u>Signs</u>

SIGNS

I always found sign regulations to be frustrating. Defining sign types, total areas of signs allowed, how many signs on a building and how many sides can they be located. Because we were in the early era of regulation, I always felt many sign regulations were not logical as were other land use regulations. Oh, and what about trucks and vehicles with prominent signs parked intentionally in front of the establishment? How do you control/regulate that so it does not get out of hand, especially if they are parked continuously to circumvent sign regulations? This probably explains why I always assigned a staff planner to be responsible for sign regulation. It's not that sign regulation and administration was not important, but as Director, I always had so many other land use regulations and decisions to deal with, along of course with many other issues.

Signs back in the day were not always aesthetically appealing and could often look, well, lousy. Today, aesthetic requirements are often implemented and coordinated on signs and buildings, as well as landscaping and other aesthetic requirements. Back in the day, we actually had a small commercial building painted Day-Glo Orange to try to stand out and attract business. That quickly caused amendments to our regulatory ordinances.

Today, it's pretty much standard and more streamlined regulations provide for much more pleasing and aesthetically desirable commercial, industrial and professional office sites.

Typically, a **Legal Nonconforming Sign** may continue to exist as long as it is used continuously as long as it continues to be an active sign, even if a new building is constructed. If the legal nonconforming sign discontinues to be used for a certain period of time, it then is just nonconforming and no longer legal and would have to be replaced with a sign conforming to current requirements.

Billboard Signs are another story. They are **Off Premise** Signs that basically are structures unto themselves, rather than **Accessory Signs** on premises of a business. I have seen these signs along Interstates that look like they are 200' high.

Sign Any structure identification, device, or any object of any nature which is displayed for purposes of advertisement, announcement, declaration, demonstration, identification, or expression or to direct attention to a person, institution, organization, activity, place, object, product or business

Sign Ordinance An ordinance that regulates the size, shape, color, and elimination of signs.

Sign, Accessory Any sign related to a business or profession conducted, or to a commodity or service sold or offered for sale, upon the premises where such sign is located.

Sign Area The entire advertising area of a sign.

Sign, Awning A sign that is mounted on or painted on or attached to an awning, canopy, or patio umbrella.

Sign, Billboard A sign is a large outdoor advertising structure typically found in high-traffic areas such as alongside busy roads.

Sign, Changeable Copy A sign designed to display multiple or changing messages whether by manual, mechanical or electronic means. Such signs are characterized by changeable letters, symbols or numerals that are not permanently affixed to the structure, framing or background allowing the letters, characters, or graphics to be modified from time to time manually or by electronic or mechanical devices. Electronically changed signs may include either electronic message boards or digital displays (which may be both be referred to as "electronic display").

Sign, Directional A sign indicating a direction or a location to which traffic, whether pedestrian or vehicular, is requested to move within the parcel for the purpose of traffic control and public safety.

Sign Face The area or display surface used for the message.

Sign, General Advertising A sign directing attention to a business, product, service or entertainment conducted, sold or offered elsewhere than upon the lot on which the sign is located.

Sign, Ground A sign with not more than two faces supported by one or more uprights, poles or braces, the lowest surface of which is four feet or less above the surface of the ground, or a sign erected on a free-standing wall or monument with a solid continuous foundation.

Sign, Illuminated A sign illuminated by electricity, gas or other artificial light, including reflecting or phosphorescent light.

Sign Lighting Device Any light, string of lights or group of lights located or arranged so as to cast illumination on a sign.

Sign, Marquee A sign attached to the underside, topside or face of a marquee roof over a walk or permanent awning.

Sign, Pole A sign with not more than two (2) faces supported wholly by a pole or poles, so as to permit passage of traffic there under.

Sign, Projecting A sign erected on or attached to the outside wall of a building and which projects out at an angle from said wall.

Sign, Roof A sign erected upon the roof of a building, all surfaces of which are located above the roof surface and do not project beyond any exterior wall of the building.

Sign, Temporary A sign that is not a permanent sign, is intended for short-term display. Temporary signs sometimes contain graphics, text, or a combination of both.

Sign, **Wall** A sign erected on, attached to, painted on the surface of, or integral with the wall of any building, located in a plane parallel to the plane of the wall, and supported by the building.

Sign, **Window** A sign painted on, attached or affixed to the interior or exterior surface of a window or door of a building, or designed to be seen through a window or door.

Sign, **Nonconforming** Any sign, legally established prior to the adoption of the Zoning Ordinance, which does not fully comply with the current regulations.

CHAPTER ELEVEN

Homeowners' Associations

Homeowners' Association Bylaws

"I think the seller will accept your offer, but the Homeowners Association will never approve that shirt."

SmartMAP.com
Intelligent Real Estate

HOMEOWNERS' ASSOCIATION (HOA)

HOAs are private associations for marketing, managing, and selling homes and lots in a subdivision. A HOA grants the developer privileged voting rights in governing the association until enough property units are sold, while allowing the developer to eventually exit financial and legal responsibility of the organization. Typically the developer will transfer ownership of the association to the homeowners after selling a predetermined number of lots.

Generally any person who wants to buy a property within the area of a **Homeowners' Association** must become a member, and therefore must obey the restrictions that often limit the owner's choices.

Most homeowner associations are incorporated, and are subject to state statutes that govern non-profit corporations and homeowner associations. State oversight of homeowner associations is minimal, and it varies from state to state.

It is important to understand the difference between Zoning Regulations, Deed Restrictions and Homeowners Association (HOA) Covenants and Restrictions. Generally, the strictest applies. For example, if the HOA allows a shed to be located within 5' of the lot line, but the Zoning requirement is 10', the Zoning requirement applies. Conversely, the opposite is true.

The same is true with Deed restrictions. Deed restrictions are not as critical today as they were and they were often implemented before there were formal Land Use controls in place. Deeds will show private roads and maintenance responsibilities of the lots taking access as well as easements affecting the property. Deeds always need to be examined.

A Real Estate agent lost his license because he assured the buyers that they could construct an 8-foot fence after buying. The HOA restrictions however, limited fence height to 6'. It is important for a Real Estate Agent to know exactly what restrictions affect a property. HOA documents are readily available and a look at the deed will quickly show Deed Restrictions for the property. And of course Zoning Regulations are public information and staffs are usually readily available to provide assistance.

HOAs will most likely have an **Architectural Review Committee** that will need to approve improvements and changes to homeowners' properties. This will include changes to the exterior of the property including additions, out buildings, fences, exterior color changes and often removal of trees. These committees help insure the standards of the community. It will keep your neighbor from painting their home Day-Glo Pink!

In addition, there will be **HOA Covenants, Conditions** and **Restrictions** as well as **Bylaws, Maintenance Obligations** and other pertinent rules and procedures. These documents will be publically recorded and referenced on the recorded development plats and surveys. When there is a conflict between local governing laws and the HOA covenants, the stricter of the two take precedent.

The sidebar outlines some important points that real estate agents must understand. Every agent involved in selling or buying in a HOA community should familiarize themselves with the HOA requirements and procedures in the community. The property owner will probably have a set of copies. Most HOAs will have a website which contains the documents as well. The sidebar refers to differences in **Zoning Regulations, Deed Restrictions** and **HOA Covenants and Restrictions**. A real estate agent should be aware of any and all of these and how they impact the property, and what the consequences can be if they don't.

A HOA will have fees or dues and an agent should know what these are. Fees need to be considered when buyers investigate purchasing, are they reasonable, how often, if at all, do they increase, etc. These fees or dues must be paid and if not, the HOA can place an assessment lien on the property which is also a cloud on the title and the house could not be sold until past dues are paid. The HOA can foreclose on the property as well. These things would need to be clarified by an attorney, but an agent should be generally aware.

Fees will vary by the types of properties. For example, I live in a mixed use community with Single-family detached homes and Townhomes. The HOA fees are higher for the townhomes than the single-family homes. More things are covered by the HOA for the townhomes. The townhomes landscaping, grass cutting, amenities and home exteriors are maintained by the HOA from the monthly fees paid by the property owners. This insures the long term viability of the townhome community and protects home values into the future. The single-family detached homes pay a lesser annual HOA fee to maintain the common areas such as parks, playgrounds, entrance landscaping and signs. Improvements to the individual properties still need to meet HOA standards.

HOA Architectural Review Committee A HOA Committee that reviews additions and improvements to homes in the community to assure compliance with the HOA Covenants and Restrictions.

HOA Covenants, Conditions, and **Restriction (CC&Rs)** A restriction on the use or development of land, or which requires affirmative actions to be performed like the payment of dues to a Homeowners Association, maintenance of common open space, etc. This is set forth in a recorded agreement, and that runs with the land and is binding upon subsequent owners of the property. When there is a conflict between local governing laws and the HOA covenants, the stricter of the two take precedent.

HOA Governance Usually HOA's are structured as private corporations or private unincorporated associations (commonly as non-profit ones). HOA's are governed by federal and state statutes applicable to corporations (or unincorporated associations if so structured), as well as the HOA's own "governing documents".

HOA Board of Directors Initially the board is composed of developer-appointed members, in order to maintain the character of the community that the developer has for it. As the percentage of ownership shifts from the developer toward owners, the corresponding percentage changes from developer-appointed members to homeowners elected at an annual meeting, and ultimately the board will consist solely of homeowner-elected members. Usually the board (or parts of it) will be elected at an annual meeting of the homeowners, as specified in the Bylaws.

HOA Management Many homeowners associations hire management companies to handle the governing duties of the association. Management services are typically divided into three categories: financial only, full management, and on-site management. Financial services typically cover administration of bank accounts, bookkeeping, assessment collection, and the HOAs budget.

HOA Bylaws Bylaws typically address rules of operation including issues like membership, annual dues, the roles and duties of the Board of Directors.

(Sample HOA Declaration of Restrictions):

<u>DECLARATION OF COVENANTS, CONDITIONS, RESTRICTIONS, MAINTENANCE OBLIGATIONS AND EASEMENTS FOR DAWSON CREEK</u>

THIS DECLARATION OF COVENANTS, CONDITIONS, RESTRICTIONS, MAINTENANCE OBLIGATIONS AND EASEMENTS FOR DAWSON CREEK (the "Declaration") is made this___ day of_____, 2009, by DAWSON CREEK PARTNERS, LLC, a Delaware limited liability company, c/o _____ (hereinafter referred to as the "Declarant").

W I T N E S S E T H :

WHEREAS, Declarant is the owner of all those certain lots, pieces or parcels of land, including residential lots and private open spaces situate in_____Hundred, Kent County, State of Delaware and being more particularly bounded and described and set forth on the Record Major Subdivision Plan for Dawson Creek Subdivision (hereinafter referred to as "Dawson Creek" and also referred to herein as the "Premises" and also sometimes referred to as the "Property"), as prepared by _____ _____ dated_____ and recorded in the Office of the Recorder of Deeds in and for Kent County, State of Delaware (the "Recorder's Office") in Plot Book , Page (the "Record Plan"); and

WHEREAS, Declarant desires to develop the Premises as depicted on the Record Plan into a residential community comprised of individual building lots on which single family detached residential dwellings are planned to be built ("Lots"), and further including additional lands identified on the Plan as "Active Open Space, Passive Open Space, Alleys, Wetlands, Stormwater

Management Area, and Stormwater Management Facility (which shall include ponding areas, swales and drainage easement areas)", all collectively referred to as "Common Areas", if any, and further including all other lands within the Premises (collectively "the Community"), if any; and

WHEREAS, the Declarant desires to provide for the preservation and enhancement of the property values, amenities, and to contribute to the personal and general health, safety and welfare of residents and owners of the Lots and to subject the Premises to the covenants, conditions, restrictions and maintenance obligations set forth in this Declaration, each and all of which is and are for the benefit of the Premises, and for each owner of a part thereof; and

WHEREAS, Declarant is desirous of imposing upon the Premises certain covenants, conditions, restrictions, maintenance obligations and easements respecting the use thereof; and

NOW, THEREFORE, THIS DECLARATION WITNESSETH:

That the Declarant hereby covenants and declares that it shall hold and stand seized of the Premises, under and subject to, and hereafter each part of, or Lot in, the Premises is and shall be held, transferred, sold, conveyed and occupied subject to the following covenants, restrictions, and easements which shall be covenants running with the land and which shall be binding upon the Declarant, its successors and assigns and all subsequent or successor Declarants, owners, occupants and visitors of the Premises.

Appendix

Appendix A: SmartMAP.com – Homepage

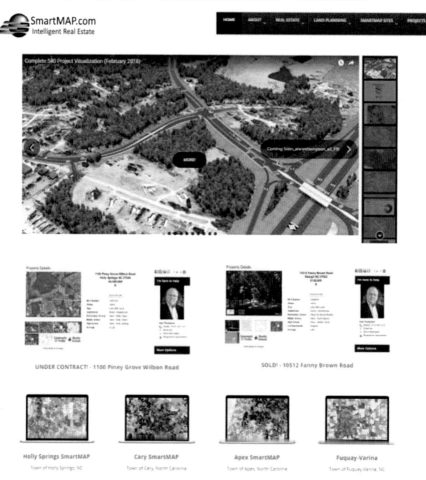

I created the SmartMAP.com website not to necessarily sell real estate, but to use as a portal, a one stop location where I could keep pertinent public information that I could use to do my job more effectively. As mentioned, most of this information is public and available on different websites, but I wanted it all in one place. In turn, it has become a helpful resource to others in my area.

I have had this website domain since the 1990's and used to use it for SmartMAP Systems we developed for clients over the years.

APPENDIX A: SMARTMAP.COM - I-540

I-540 Orange Route

Complete 540
(Click on the Map Graphic to go to the PDF of Each Map)

The map above is the index map. It shows the different map pages of proposed construction by page number. Select the page number you want a closer look at below.

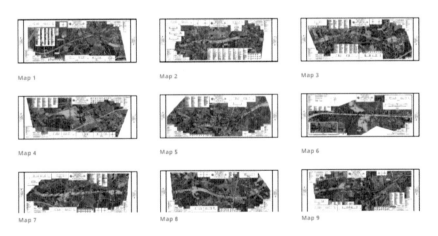

I-540 is an Interstate loop around Raleigh, NC. This section, the Orange Route, is the final portion to be built. The maps shown come from NCDOT and show the detailed alignment. These maps are downloadable and the eBook below the maps show impacted subdivisions.

APPENDIX A: SMARTMAP.COM - LAND PLANNING SERVICES

Land Planning Services

I also provide **Land Planning Services** to my clients free of charge as part of my **Value Added Service** as a **Real Estate Broker**. Like any other Broker, I get paid by commission, and in addition I do not charge extra for these **Planning Consulting Services**.

Consulting Services: I council and advise my clients in examining the highest and best use for the property, whether selling or buying.

Site Analysis (Preliminary): I provide a preliminary site analysis looking at physical and environmental characteristics that affect the property. This includes property assessment information, zoning, soils, wetlands, topography, etc.

Rezoning Services: If a rezoning is required, I will, if requested, consult and coordinate the rezoning effort. If it is a straight forward rezoning, I may handle the rezoning all the way through the process. If it a more complicated matter, I will consult throughout the process in the event a lawyer is required to present the rezoning at public hearing. I do not provide legal, surveying or engineering services, but will coordinate these services on behalf of my clients.

Minor Subdivision Services: In the event where my client wants to create a minor subdivision (no streets) and the local jurisdiction allows, I will coordinate the process to completion. I will provide a sketch plan and preliminary site analysis. If approved by the local authority, I'll coordinate the surveyor's submission, etc.

As part of my Value-Added real estate service as a Broker, I offer Planning Consulting. Many residential clients who are simply purchasing an existing house, these services for the most part are not required, other than the importance of being a knowledgeable Real Estate Agent. But a client buying a vacant lot for development, this is critical. It is also important for commercial clients.

APPENDIX A: SMARTMAP.COM - HOLLY SPRINGS SMARTMAP SITE

SmartMAP.com has several website pages specific to areas where I primarily focus my efforts. Many of these links are to maps including GIS and other public maps. There are also additional links to each area in the SmartMAP.com footer available on every page of the website.

Appendix B: SmartMAP.com - Holly Springs SmartMAP

This is a GIS (Geographic Information System) SmartMAP. I have one on my website for each area that I work in. This is public information that is online, but I prefer have this on my website and I put it in a form that I find easier to use. It basically has the information most pertinent to me rather than all the data that may be available.

There are layers that can be turned off and on as desired. Some more congested layers may only turn on a certain view elevations. For example, Parcels may only turn on when zooming into a certain level. Layers include Parcels linked to Assessment Data, Zoning, Soils, Flood Prone Areas, Topography and others.

APPENDIX C: FACEBOOK - ZONING 101 FOR REAL ESTATE AGENTS

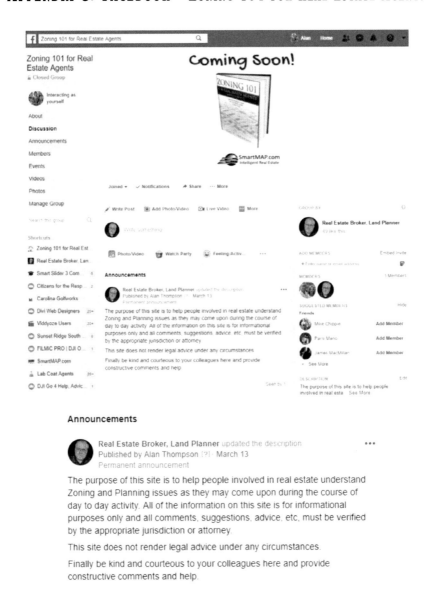

Announcements

Real Estate Broker, Land Planner updated the description
Published by Alan Thompson [?] · March 13
Permanent announcement

The purpose of this site is to help people involved in real estate understand Zoning and Planning issues as they may come upon during the course of day to day activity. All of the information on this site is for informational purposes only and all comments, suggestions, advice, etc, must be verified by the appropriate jurisdiction or attorney.

This site does not render legal advice under any circumstances.

Finally be kind and courteous to your colleagues here and provide constructive comments and help.

This is a Facebook Group that I've created for this book. It's not just to sell the book, but it is hoped it can be an asset to Real Estate Agents and others who could benefit from some Zoning and Land Use help. It is a closed group so it's not open to those who may have no interest. The announcement is a pinned post that will always be the first thing people see when joining the group.

APPENDIX D: FACEBOOK - REAL ESTATE BROKER, LAND PLANNER

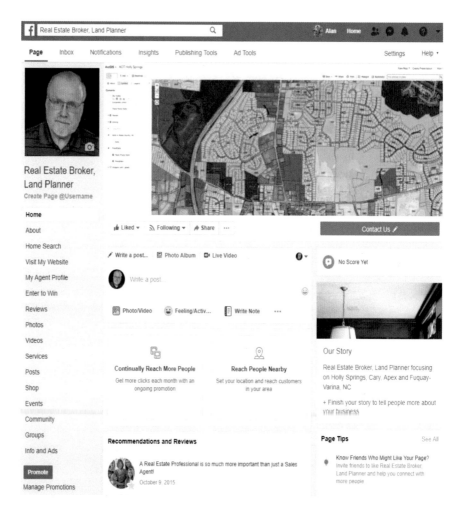

This is my Business Facebook Page. I used to post to it more often when I worked for a different Broker. I'm now an Independent Broker. The page is still useful and, of course, is Real Estate related. I used this page to create the Zoning 101 for Real Estate Agents Facebook Page. So it is linked this page and my Personal Facebook Page.

Appendix E: FEMA – Flood Insurance Rate Map (FIRM)

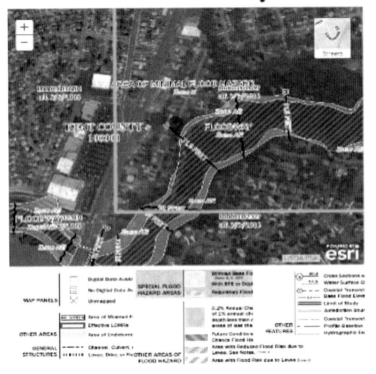

This is a graphic that is in Chapter Two and is a Flood Insurance Rate Map (FIRM). This and the following two pages represent paperwork from FEMA on a personal situation I found myself in. I refer to it in a sidebar also in Chapter Two.

The house we owned at the time is where the red marker is in the graphic. This resulted in a Letter of Map Amendment (LOMA) which is referred to in the paperwork as a Letter of Map Revision (LOMR) in the paperwork. Basically it's what I had to go through to prove that I was not in a Floodway and did not need Federal Flood Insurance.

APPENDIX E: FEMA – LETTER OF MAP AMENDMENT (LOMA)
PAGE 1

Page 1 of 2		Date: October 12, 2004	Case No.: 04-03-1410A	LOMR-FW

Federal Emergency Management Agency
Washington, D.C. 20472

LETTER OF MAP REVISION FLOODWAY
DETERMINATION DOCUMENT (REMOVAL)

COMMUNITY AND MAP PANEL INFORMATION		LEGAL PROPERTY DESCRIPTION
COMMUNITY	CITY OF DOVER, KENT COUNTY, DELAWARE	Lot 88 and a tract adjacent to Lot 88, Taylor Estate, as described in Corporate Deed, Document No. 05520, recorded in Book T44, Pages 301 and 302, filed on March 21, 1988, by the Recorder of Deeds, Kent County, Delaware
	COMMUNITY NO.: 100006	
AFFECTED MAP PANEL	NUMBER: 10001C0169H	
	NAME: KENT COUNTY, DELAWARE AND INCORPORATED AREAS	
	DATE: 05/05/2003	

FLOODING SOURCE: ISAAC BRANCH; MOORES LAKE	APPROXIMATE LATITUDE & LONGITUDE OF PROPERTY: 39.127, -75.528
	SOURCE OF LAT & LONG: PRECISION MAPPING STREETS 6.0 DATUM: NAD 83

DETERMINATION

LOT	BLOCK/ SECTION	SUBDIVISION	STREET	OUTCOME WHAT IS REMOVED FROM THE SFHA	FLOOD ZONE	1% ANNUAL CHANCE FLOOD ELEVATION (NAVD 88)	LOWEST ADJACENT GRADE ELEVATION (NAVD 88)	LOWEST LOT ELEVATION (NAVD 88)
—	—	Taylor Estate	1727 South Taylor Drive	Residential Structure	X (unshaded)	11.5 feet	—	—

Special Flood Hazard Area (SFHA) - The SFHA is an area that would be inundated by the flood having a 1-percent chance of being equaled or exceeded in any given year (base flood).

ADDITIONAL CONSIDERATIONS (Please refer to the appropriate section on Attachment 1 for the additional considerations listed below.)

INADVERTENT INCLUSION IN FLOODWAY 1
ANNEXATION

This document provides the Federal Emergency Management Agency's determination regarding a request for a Letter of Map Revision for the property described above. Using the information submitted and the effective National Flood Insurance Program (NFIP) map, we have determined that the structure(s) on the property(ies) is/are not located in the NFIP regulatory floodway or the SFHA, an area inundated by the flood having a 1-percent chance of being equaled or exceeded in any given year (base flood). This document revises the effective NFIP map to remove the subject property from the NFIP regulatory floodway and the SFHA located on the effective NFIP map; therefore the Federal mandatory flood insurance requirement does not apply. However, the lender has the option to continue the flood insurance requirement to protect its financial risk on the loan. A Preferred Risk Policy (PRP) is available for buildings located outside the SFHA. Information about the PRP and how one can apply is enclosed.

This determination is based on the flood data presently available. The enclosed documents provide additional information regarding this determination. If you have any questions about this document, please contact the FEMA Map Assistance Center toll free at (877) 336-2627 (877-FEMA MAP) or by letter addressed to the Federal Emergency Management Agency, P.O. Box 2210, Merrifield, VA 22116-2210. Additional information about the NFIP is available on our web site at http://www.fema.gov/nfip/.

Doug Bellomo, P.E., CFM, Acting Chief
Hazard Identification Section, Mitigation Division
Emergency Preparedness and Response Directorate

Version 1.3.4

62175103 0301126116Y0E00003011261

Index

A

Access Easement, 66
Administrative Review, 31
Agricultural Preservation Program, 27
Airport Flight Impact, 21
Alley, Private, 61
Alley, Public, 61
Appendix, 89
Architectural Review Committee, 85

B

Board of Adjustment, 30
Boundary Survey, 30
Buffer, 71
Buffer Zone, 71
Buildable Area, 47
Building Code, 21
Building Permit, 21

C

Certificate for a Sign, 20
Certificate of Occupancy, 21
Child Day-Care Center, 42
Comprehensive Land Use Plan, 42
Conditional Use, 17
Condominium, 55
Council, 31

D

Development Advisory Committee (DAC), 32
Development Rights, 32
Development Rights, Transfer of (TDR), 32
Duplex Home, 55

E

Easement, 66

T

U

Use, Permitted, 40
Use, Principal (Primary), 41
Use, Secondary, 41
Use, Temporary, 40

V

Variance, 30

W

Waste Water Treatment Plant, 74
Wetlands, 30
Wetlands, Freshwater, 30

Y

Yard, Buffer, 71
Yard, Front, 48
Yard, Rear, 48
Yard, Side, 48

Z

Zero Lot Line Home, 53
Zoning, 14
Zoning Certificate, 20
Zoning Department, 20
Zoning Inspector, 20
Zoning Ordinance, 19
Zoning, Aesthetic, 19

Made in the USA
Middletown, DE
15 July 2018